SHE WAS HERE, AND HER EYES WERE BROWN

Alicia Marchetti

SHE WAS HERE, AND HER EYES WERE BROWN

ISBN 979-8-218-83888-1

Illustrations by Andriy Dankovych.
(licensed for commercial use)

For permissions or inquiries, contact:
HerEyesWereBrown@protonmail.com

Printed in the United States of America.
First Edition, 2026.

Hers, forever.

CONTENTS

DEDICATED TO HAZEL BROWN

AUTHOR'S NOTE

This began with a girl I met when we were both still becoming.

Now that we are women, I write this for her, and for the love that still lives within me.

These pages are my way of honoring what is—and has always been—real.

I offer this collection with unwavering devotion, reverence, and the hope that wherever she is, she is touched by it.

Over the course of a year, I have destroyed and restored these pieces more times than I can count, always with her in mind.

This collection is not without its flaws. You may find errors here and there.

I am not a genius, and I never wrote this to be a bestseller. It was achieved through love and commitment, and the only recognition I hope for is hers.

My intention in sharing this publicly is to create

something lasting, for her and for myself. A grand gesture, if you will.

This collection may not adhere to every rule, but it is human and true.

X☺X+X☺X
Alicia

REDEEM

I reach for her again—
the woman who makes me feel alive.

I am rebuilding myself—
hoping she sees the effort
and feels the love in every step.

I search for moments of grace
to prove
this is a safe place
for her heart.

UNTITLED

Between the devil
and the deep blue sea.

I remind myself
that this life
is
transitory.

That thought comforts me,
yet fills me with an urgent need
to be with
the one I love.

I VISUALIZE HER EYES

I visualize her eyes
in countless ways,
umber nights
and amber days.

Moss on oak,
chocolate truffle,
tobacco.

Brandy
with all the words
I wish she would want to know.

While I am engulfed
in this symphony of hues,

how could she ever think
I would find someone new?

All these colors—
but still, too vaguely.

I visualize her eyes
to keep them from fading.

SITTING WITH IT

From my eyes,
shortcomings spill,

and they shape my perspective.

Hopeless, flowing streams
of iridescence.

To return to your persistence,
to behave more... appropriately...
in my adolescence.

You are my sun.

Without you, the light here is
f l u o r e s c e n t.

AMERICAN DREAM

You are my American Dream.

Glutenfree, countryfried
saffron sunset—VICTORY.

I miss your strong arms.
I know what was real.

I forgive you if you forgive me.

UNTIL YOU ARRIVE

Come as you are,

breathless and bruised,
starlit and splitting,
pressed like flowers.

I will still call you beautiful.

NASCAR hummingbirds
and leaf-shutter butterflies
will keep me company
until you arrive.

FIREWORKS

Watching you, I saw the woman I had dreamed of marrying since I was a little girl. Zeus struck me for glancing your way. I was young and unaware, and your side profile glowed when that red stoplight touched your skin and lit up your hair. Your radiance washed over me, awakening and erasing me at the same time. Your beauty was impossible for me to comprehend, and it felt both familiar and foreign, unexpected and unfair. It was immediately undoing, the moment was fleeting, but I tried my best not to stare.

NOTE TO HAZEL BROWN:
Suddenly, you looked different. You still look... different.

LOCKED IN

Custom frames are worth the effort
when what they surround is you.

I would take mosquitoes over dragonflies
if it meant we were in the same room.

I do not chase,
but I am a dog,
and you are the news.

They say people have types.
I don't know.
I just have you.

Only a single June beetle amid billions of locusts.

PURPOSE

The world is huge, and I am small—
insignificant.

But I am not hollow.
I am weightless.

I am not adrift.
I am driven.

I cannot wait to secure my wife and children—

go to work,
cook dinner,
and show my sons
how to treat their mother
with gentleness and awe.

A WORLD WE MADE

I envision a future
where flower arrangements
are debated like war,

clutched in tiny hands,
sunlit and feral,
beneath the sycamores.

You come home, weary,
see their arms full of color,
and find peace.

I soften the lights.

We settle into a movie,
your head on my chest,
my hand in your hair.

Our kids are whole,
resting in a world
ever kind.

A world we made.

If I choose to rest in your arms,
no threat—real or imagined—can cross
that threshold.

UNTITLED

Hazel Brown,

Another November white jasmine need not bloom.
My folly-holy heart, veins, vines themselves,
sustain this body, which I have freely given to you.
I fear that old-fashioned love is a thing of the past.
Can one woman love another in such a way?

Yours,
A

YOU ARE

You are a starling, a black bat flower,
a cappuccino before noon, every tidal phase,
sweat-soaked linen, a Tahitian pearl,
and the smell of rain.

The lawn of the amphitheater
where we once sat,
sound reverberating,
Coca-Cola mixed with rum,
the dragonflies in my stomach,
and a child holding a starfish at an aquarium.

You are chivalrous, sensitive, strong—
rich soil, a double rainbow,
ebony and opium.

You are warm feet in winter,
virgin snow,
a weeping willow
reflecting its image off a lake,

a meadow of baby's breath,
an olive branch,
a mountain of magnolia leaves
neatly raked.

You are a white picket fence that never decays.

You are the gentle tap that breaks the crème brûlée.

You, come back to me, okay?

BOUGAINVILLEA ARMS

I want to hold your hand,

maybe trace my thumb
around and across
your palm.

I want you most
when it's cold
or dark,

held—tangled and tender
in my bougainvillea
arms.

THIN AIR

You run hot.
We make sense.

Warm people
belong together
in the mountains
at Christmastime.

MONSOON

A damp sigh,
a respite from this season's golden wrath.

On Grand Avenue,
a baker's dozen of palm trees
climb the street.

And right now,
the sky looks like berries.

I look up and wonder:
do your heather-lavender eyes
ever wander
to that boysenberry-jam sky?

Do storms frighten you?
When it thunders,
does it shake you too?

Do you tense
and pause?

And in that pause,
do you think of me at all?

PARKED

I never thought I would end up anywhere
but here—

in the stillness of this parking lot,
contemplating my existence
on this forever-turning sphere.

Some things never change.

I might be driving a different car,
but I am still parked in the same space.

Sure, I could be with somebody else,
but I would only ever see your face.

Saltwater taffy, mambas, and Hi-Chews...

PISTACHIOS

Parker, Arizona,
a paradise she shared with me,
dry heat and serenity,
and I was whole.

I still feel the life vest against my chest.

I let my cheek nestle into her shoulder
as we sped down the Colorado River,
and I held onto her.

Dragonflies raced beside us,
their wings a blur,
and the homes along the river's edge
sparked visions of a forever
that looked just like this.

The sun on my skin,
her body against mine—
melding, inseparable.

ASTRO ORBITER

A Disney rocket,
where I asked you to be mine.

You won me in line.

LET ME

In the ocean's green room,
I am going to ride this out.

Still in that honeymoon glow,
these backroads are striking.

I would rather not reroute.

Please, let me be in love with you.
Let me be loud.

Let me ride this wave
like it will never crash down.

SPILL

I am d

        o

           w

    n,

    d

     o

       w

           n,

       d

         o

           w

        n.

Please, honey, reassure me
that I am in the right place,

like the bees who feed on date palm
blossoms.

Even when I stumble, because I will,
may I ask
for your strong hands
to cradle my face?

Tell me to look at you,
and I swear
I will.

I will stare into those big, hazel eyes
till my cup runneth over
and
spill.

TRANSCENDENT

Her hair cascades
in jasmine waves.

Her eon-patina eyes
watch butterflies and bees
flit between flowers.

Helios casts sunbeams
upon her honeyed Celtic skin...

Yet, she is untouched.

For she is the sun incarnate.

SUPERNOVA

Her
    eyes
        shelter
            all the collapsed stars
                that space
                    could not hold
                    in its
                        dark.

I lost an invaluable photo of us on I-5 northbound
when I rolled the window down.

OMENS

She, with clipped wings and southern charm,
calls me "pretty girl,"
says I have her attention.

But on my way to work,
a hawk landed on a lamppost
in front of my car,
and it just stared at me.

Days later, by the lake,
as I pondered the universe
and its signs,
I thought of you—
you, the woman with multicolored eyes.

Then suddenly, a dragonfly appeared,
level with my gaze,
and it just stared at me.

Note to Hazel Brown:
The signs are never loud, but they always point to you.

CAMELLIAS

If palm trees are rats' nests
and roses are twice as ugly,

what, then, is good enough for you?

You will probably dismiss this poem, too.

You think she is beautiful,
even though she makes you blue,

and I am just an errand
you do not want to do.

For the record,
I do not like roses much either.

But mine bloom like camellias
compared to the flowers she brings you.

SPLINTERS

Marrow bones simmer
as I write this letter.

I am wearing patchouli musk—
an oil perfume.

Your proclamations pierce me,
my heart **sp**
  lin
    ter
     s.

DISARM

Are you my revival
or my rival?

Can I rest here safely
without my revolver?

FROOT LOOPS

I told you I would not wear
cheap jewelry.

I know I can be entitled,
but you make me nervous.

Admittedly,

I would wear a necklace
made of string
and Froot Loops,

if you gave it to me.

MAKE A WISH

Fresh, cream-top milk in glass bottles.
Cushions, spread in the bed of a truck.
Winding mountain roads,
chicken piccata,
cheap motels,
and jet skis at full throttle.

Casinos, farmers markets,
groceries at the store.
Parking lots, bedrooms,
four squeezes—
a silent way of saying, "I love you more."

Botanic Park,
picnic bench,
peanut butter cup,
mustard-fried,
Oceanside,
you by my side.

Windows down,
country songs blaring.

We passed sheep and goats,
vineyards, orchards,
homesteads.

Today I turned twenty-seven.
Someone said, "Make a wish."

I smiled,
thinking:

I already did.

MERCY

She
   asks
   for nothing

but mercy,

            warmth
                  in human

            form.

The ocean behind you competed for my attention,
but it failed.

DOMESTIC BLISS

It is getting dark.
I am folding the laundry.

I imagine you in the living room,
on the couch.

You would be watching a movie,
your eyes,
Disney-drowsy.

I would bring in the comforters,
still warm from the dryer,
and lay them over you gently
because it is the best feeling.

And that is all.
That is love,
after all.

WOULD YOU GO WITH ME?

In Julian, California, there is a farm-to-table restaurant. Across the street is a farm and orchard with a sign out front that reads, "Pick berries and flowers." It is perfect because there is an inn nearby, and the rooms do not have TVs.

We could go there afterward, once we've grown tired, our baskets full and lazily carried. We could cover the bed in petals from our bouquets, take a long, hot bath and feed each other fresh-picked fruit until checkout the next day.

I want to give you my full attention and make you feel okay.

Through the grapevine, I heard about a little winery. I'm a sucker for a good red, the weather couldn't be better, and you are so pretty.

Hazel Brown, what do you think? Would you go with me?

NOTE TO HAZEL BROWN:
Call me.

GAIA AND SELENE

Your memory is gravity,
and I,
orbit endlessly.

You must be Gaia,
and I,
Selene.

I am forever falling,
despite space,
toward you—

inevitably.

WEATHERED
AND SUN-WORN

Whether you are present or not,
when the sun emerges
and I am unoccupied,

I step outside
to the furniture—weathered and sun-worn—

and unfailingly,

I think of you.

I want you to know
that that first kiss meant
the whole wide world to me.

DARK KISS

When I ache,
I spray it,
and you return.

So close.
So impossibly close.

As if I could reach for you
the way I once did
so effortlessly.

I want you,
not as a fantasy,
but here,
whole,
real,

and in my arms once again.

THE FAMINE OUR FERVOR BECAME

Where breath becomes prayer,
you linger,
every poem is your name.

The silence is strangling
where your voice should be.

To taste you in time,
where we exist
still.

Kisses left in the ether—

intangible.

THE MEMORY ROOM

The everyday rhythm of her brushing her teeth.
The nearly nonexistent weight of her footsteps.
The way she gathers her hair, lost in thought—
unaware she is everything.

Though she is not here, the house still breathes,
alive with her memory,
because she is alive in mine.

And as long as I breathe in this room,
so too will she.

OPTIONS

I can bring you ice cream,
frozen solid,
or softened.

Fresh-cut flowers each week,
or seeds we scatter together
in the garden.

We can live in the suburbs,
the countryside,
the desert,
or a city flat.

I can support you in your passions,
in your education,
in building a home,
all of it.

Choose the religion for our family.
I respect them all.

The names of our children,
and where they go to school.

I can entertain you:
a romance,
a drama,
a comedy.

I can read you:

poems,
novels,
short stories,
and finally,

our autobiography.

I hope tonight's sunset suffuses the sky
with a rich blend of orange-red—your color.

GET TO KNOW ME

Strong-willed,
pretty, pretty woman
foresees the undertow.

Test the water.
Let's go slow.

Sweet sap flows
from maple trees
in abundance
(once they mature).

Get to know me for my soul,
get to know me,
get to know me for my soul.

Let's take a cutting
from the eucalyptus,
then propagate it.

Let's follow its lead—
climb towards the light,

G R O W.

Get to know me,
get to know me for my soul,
get to know me.

Meet me at Lestat's in the middle of the night.

MAIDEN NAME

Inside my father's rib cage,
there is a cherry-red Mustang.

My mother's heart is a sweet violet.

Their colors blend so beautifully;
I doubt she misses her maiden name.

NOTE TO HAZEL BROWN:
Neither will I.

PARADISE

Tornadoes go in circles.
Pink flamingos stand in place.

A bouquet from the local florist waits,
lonely in its porcelain vase.

If I had loved that devil,
don't you think I would have kissed her more
gently?

Truly, Hazel Brown,
you are the only woman I see.

In my heart,
we are driving to El Cajon in your car,

where we will sit in a park
beyond the trees,

sipping sangria,

and laughing for eternity.

HANDS, HEART, CROWN

Your parents invited me to dinner.

"Eat the frog," I thought.
I had spent breakfast and lunch
entwined in nerves.

You looked so pretty in white.
You were impressive,
without a doubt,
more mature.

A decade has passed since then,
and still,
you are the most beautiful woman in the world.

I knew they wanted the best for you.
I knew I looked absurd.

The ribs were sweet, savory, and tender—
proof of your parents' labor.

I was there.
I loved you.
I wanted to win their favor.
A young woman—
unrealized,
unknowing,
careful not to misstep.

Though I now realize

that my faults might have gone unnoticed,
had I eaten without fear,
allowing the sauce
to messily cover them.

NOTE TO HAZEL BROWN (AND FAMILY):
Please forgive me for being so late.

UNTITLED

      Kindnesses linger
longer than morning glories.
      A bad
impression loiters
        like a poorly told story.

A FRAGMENT OF A LETTER
TO HER FATHER

I think the world of your daughter, and with
good reason.

My affection for her is not random; it is the
result of my deepest beliefs and aspirations.

She exemplifies the virtues I admire. She is
strong and sensitive, and—respectfully, sir—
the most beautiful woman I have ever seen.
She is ambitious, composed, intelligent, and
childlike. She is remarkable and rare, and she
keeps me grounded.

I wholeheartedly believe she can do anything,
and I want nothing more than to spend my life
by her side.

BLUR

In that unreal place, the limbo between
consciousness and nonbeing, I dreamed.

A world without you unfurled, a forced bloom.
Solitary, sterile—a realm steeped in longing
and despair.

Too vivid to deny, too final to reverse. What
was done was done. I came home to silence—to
confines empty of you.

One night, as I stood alone in the dim light of my
apartment, I saw the lamp. Its glow faltered, its
edges wavered—twisting like heat on pavement.
For a moment, everything was still. My vision
blurred—the dream shattered.

I woke up. The light above me was real. The air felt
borrowed—filtered, thin, foreign. The monitors'
steady beeping guided me to the surface. Then
I felt your warm, steady hand holding mine. I
turned and saw you. Pain collapsed, like paper
burning to ash.

Your eyes shimmered, relief spilling like sunlight
after rain. Your achingly beautiful face, framed
in a tenderness I thought I had lost forever. I had
not lost you after all. You had never left me. The
breakup, the silence, the life I thought I lived

without you—none of it was real. It was only a cruel dream.

I said your name, barely breathing, afraid I was still dreaming. Your smile trembled as though you had been waiting for years. Then, with infinite gentleness and certainty, you kissed me, pulling me into reality—into you.

Everything dissolved, and what remained was us.

You were real.
You loved me.
I was home.

1

Marchetti

2

3

Marchetti

PLAYLIST

"I Will Always Return," by Bryan Adams

"All of Me," by John Legend

"I'm on Fire," by Bruce Springsteen

"Whatever It Is," by Zac Brown Band

"Fade Away," by Rebelution

"We Are on Time," by Nahko and Medicine for
the People

"Ghost," by Justin Bieber

"Pink Skies (Demo)," by Wiley from Atlanta

"Can't Help Falling in Love," by Elvis Presley

"Losin Control," by Russ

"A Drop in the Ocean," by Ron Pope

"Wait for You," by Elliott Yamin

"I Won't Back Down," by Tom Petty

"Great Gatsby," by Rod Wave

"Watercolours," by Philip Lewin

"Dear Miss," by Zach Bryan

"A Song for You," by Leon Russell

"Hallelujah," by Leonard Cohen

"All I See Is You," by Shane Smith & the Saints

Marchetti

WATCHLIST

1883. Season 1, Episode 5, "The Fangs of Freedom."

Anne with an E. Season 2, Episode 7, "Memory Has as Many Moods as the Temper."

Black Mirror. Season 7, Episode 5, "Eulogy."

The Last of Us. Season 1, Episode 3, "Long, Long Time."

Marchetti

ACKNOWLEDGMENTS

What a thing to bleed for! What a relief it is to be able to bleed at all!

I love you all. I love love.

I am profoundly grateful for my time on earth in this mortal body, for every feeling Hazel Brown allowed me, and for the gift of free will, which enables me to step outside and behold the sun.

With deep appreciation, I wish to acknowledge my parents for every opportunity, and my God, for entrusting me with hands, a heart, and eyes.

Through these invaluable gifts, I have been able to create, learn, love, lose, and truly live. For them, I remain eternally very, very grateful.

X☺X+X☺X
Alicia